# In My Tummy

# Teaching Tips

## Yellow Level 3

This book focuses on the phonemes /ch/sh/.

## Before Reading

- Discuss the title. Ask readers what they think the book will be about.
- Sound out the words on page 3 together.

## Read the Book

- Ask readers to use a finger to follow along with each word as it is read.
- Encourage readers to break down unfamiliar words into units of sound. Then, ask them to string the sounds together to create the words.
- Urge readers to point out when the focused phonics phonemes appear in the text.

## After Reading

- Encourage children to reread the book independently or with a friend.
- Guide readers through the phonics exercises at the end of the book.

---

© 2024 Booklife Publishing
This edition is published by arrangement with Booklife Publishing.

North American adaptations © 2024 Jump!
5357 Penn Avenue South
Minneapolis, MN 55419
www.jumplibrary.com

Decodables by Jump! are published by Jump! Library.
All rights reserved. No part of this book may be reproduced in any form without written permission from the publisher.

Library of Congress Cataloging-in-Publication Data is available at www.loc.gov or upon request from the publisher.

ISBN: 979-8-88524-721-4 (hardcover)
ISBN: 979-8-88524-722-1 (paperback)
ISBN: 979-8-88524-723-8 (ebook)

## Photo Credits

Images are courtesy of Shutterstock.com. With thanks to Getty Images, Thinkstock Photo and iStockphoto. Cover – Shutterstock. p4–5 – Syda Productions, RasaBasa. p6–7 – Tyler Olson, StockImageFactory.com. p8–9 – M-Production, JenJPayless. p10–11 – RecycleMan, New Africa. p15 – Shutterstock.

Can you find these words in the book?

chips

chop

mashed

Chop chop. Mom and Dad chop to fill my tummy.

I can dip chips to go in my tummy.

Chocolate chips are good in my tummy. Yum!

Mashed potatoes can be fun.
Fun mashed potatoes in my tummy.

It will be a salad. A salad in my tummy.

Roll roll roll. It will go in my tummy.

She fills up her tummy. Yum yum yum!

Yum and fun. It is yummy in my tummy.

# Can you say these sounds and draw them with your finger?

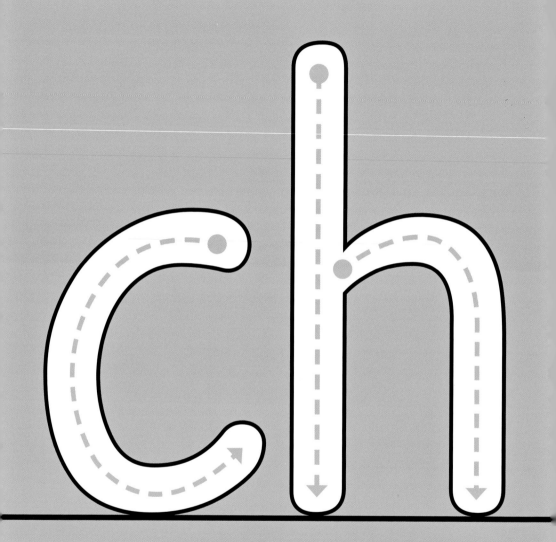

Trace the missing letters to finish these words:

chips

chop

mashed

What other words do you know with the sounds /ch/ or /sh/?

cheer

cheese

shark

shoes

## Practice reading the book again:

Chop chop. Mom and Dad chop to fill my tummy.

I can dip chips to go in my tummy.

Chocolate chips are good in my tummy. Yum!

Mashed potatoes can be fun.
Fun mashed potatoes in my tummy.

It will be a salad. A salad in my tummy.

Roll roll roll. It will go in my tummy.

She fills up her tummy. Yum yum yum!

Yum and fun. It is yummy in my tummy.